CARNATIONS

PRINCETON SERIES OF CONTEMPORARY POETS

Paul Muldoon, *series editor*

CARNATIONS

Poems

Anthony Carelli

PRINCETON UNIVERSITY PRESS

Princeton & Oxford

PS3603.A736 C37 2011
Carelli, Anthony, 1979–
Carnations : poems
Princeton, N.J. : Princeton
University Press, c2011.

Published by Princeton University Press, 41 William Street,
Princeton, New Jersey 08540

In the United Kingdom: Princeton University Press, 6 Oxford Street,
Woodstock, Oxfordshire OX20 1TW

press.princeton.edu

Jacket art: Pieter Bruegel the Elder, *Christ Carrying the Cross* (1564).
Courtesy of Kunsthistorisches Museum, Vienna.

LIBRARY OF CONGRESS CATALOGING-IN-PUBLICATION DATA
Carelli, Anthony, 1979–
  Carnations : poems / Anthony Carelli.
    p. cm. — (Princeton series of contemporary poets)
  ISBN 978-0-691-14944-8 (cloth : alk. paper) — ISBN 978-0-691-14945-5
  (pbk : alk. paper)
  I. Title.
  PS3603.A736C37 2011
  811'.6—dc22   2010035406

British Library Cataloging-in-Publication Data is available

This book has been composed in Adobe Garamond

Printed on acid-free paper. ∞

Printed in the United States of America

10 9 8 7 6 5 4 3 2 1

Acknowledgments

Thanks to the editors of the following publications in which some of these poems first appeared, often in different versions: *AGNI, Memorious, The New Yorker, Slice*, and *Washington Square*.

A few of these poems also appeared along with translations by Rodrigo Rojas in *Cinco Poems, Five Poemas*, a beautiful chapbook published by Epistola Press, in Santiago, Chile.

My greatest thanks to my family: Jim Carelli, Robin Carelli, and Anne Carelli. And to my fellow poets: Wynelle Bridge, Jordan Davidoff, Angie Gius, Kathleen Graber, Sarah Heller, and Amy Hosig. And to my teachers: Mark Doty, Melissa Hammerle, Philip Levine, and Tom Sleigh.

Contents

How fresh, O Lord, how sweet and clean
Are Thy returns.

—George Herbert, *The Flower*

Carnations, those marvelous rags.
How clean they are.

—Francis Ponge, *The Carnation*

CARNATIONS

THE SABBATH

We weren't speaking. It was snowing, temps dipping
into the teens. You and I were playing Frisbee
because we'd fought all day, and it's a tonic
to get outside and throw the sharp disk at one another
with cold dumb hands. Then the animals appeared.
Horses—male, I think—a pair of grayish steeds climbed
the man-cleared path to the softball field
in Prospect Park, where we stood at a distance.
"Wow:" you said, "horses," but I missed them at first.
I was chasing down the disk that overshot, banked
above and hissed in the sky, a flattened apple.
I had had it. "Baby," I almost said, "I'm *trying*
to make a catch here." But I was stopped instead,
lofted like the Frisbee. It was the word *horses*
in Brooklyn air. It was their bodies in Brooklyn in 2007.
Though what is the good of horses in Brooklyn in 2007?
As the first came he bowed his head with one step
and hoisted with the next, nodding like a drunk to nobody
he knows; so slowly that, within the machinations
of a single nod, I revised this scene a dozen times
and made a fine behind-the-back Frisbee snatch
to boot. And yes, I remembered the horses of Achilles,
the chariot of Israel, and Emily's toward Eternity . . .
Sometime I'd like to discuss the horses at length.
Meanwhile the second horse did whatever I say
the first horse did, which is walk, and smoke breath,
glimmer and gloom. They both shouldered through
the intermittent aeons of twilight as mitigated

by black tree shafts. There were riders, too—
there must have been. They wore fancy sweaters—
red, or was it blue? I even thought to go to them,
gently, and stare into their eyes (the horses, I mean)
to see the candles on the horse-shaped altar inside—
horses are, perhaps, more lovely than a Frisbee
—but that's not what happened, Honey. This
is our life: we fought until dark, we mastered
our timing, you made that magnificent cartwheel toss.

GLASS WORK SONG

Well, he was no theologian,
but when we were children
my best friend's father would speak of the lord,
though only when given a question,
so we asked him often.
                                Otherwise
his cantos were carried by a foreman's voice
so unlike our own—volume high
to overcall the furnace howl, tone low
to part and cross the shriek
of those conveyors he left at five,
and the shattered eardrum he didn't.

But ask of Golgotha,
ask of the Good Samaritan,
and the great voice slowed, faltered,
bent, and broke finally, grunting to carry
the words of the lord. *Grace, Angel,*
Nazareth, Rome—disparate notes
of a fractured tune
                                gathered
in dinnertime steam. Rising
over beans, beets, venison chuck,
a melody hummable by none of us
was nonetheless hummed by all.

And so it was for my friend
in his twenty-second year.

He set out quiet from the Windy City
six months early, out of cash,
out from the school of his choice
to the job he'd sworn he'd never do.
This song: his father's job. This song:
the glass plant.
                    And so it was
that Wednesday, hump day,
his third day of work.
He began to sing nonetheless.
Over coffee mugs and cigarettes
on picnic tables, among men mid-
break in a brick wall room,
he raised his voice.
                    It sounded like this:
Couldn't we go faster if we lifted alone?
Isn't this tri-pane impossible to shatter?
—not good beginnings.

Whoever you are, you aren't surprised
how quickly, sharply, the men, in response,
said nothing at all.
                    How glancingly
they spoke about the sheets and sheets
they'd stacked six days a week
for years—always *two men* to a pane.
This song is not about materials.
This song is how to pick and swing
an eight-foot length without decapitating
Bruce or Joe. Among them, this song
is not knowing glass. Lifting it? Yes.
Carrying? Balancing?
Yes.
            But those ponderous rectangle
hushes of air, those reflective spans
they won't lift alone? Daily they sing
one another this omittance. Each will have

the next
        enjoy this *Grace, Angel,*
Nazareth . . . They are in attendance
to the music—
            scales heard, day in,
day out, in common; a lifetime
of tickets to La Scala, but knowing
there's no need to leave Kenosha.
To stack these panes for many years
and say very little of glass:

this is fellowship among them
becoming fellowship
among us, a chorus that aspires
to a certain quiet; a quiet becoming
the closest we can get.

THE PROPHETS

A river. And if not the river nearby, then a dream
  of a river. Nothing happens that doesn't happen
    along a river, however humble the water may be.

Take Rowan Creek, the trickle struggling to lug
  its mirroring across Poynette, wherein, suspended,
    so gentle and shallow, I learned to walk, bobbing

at my father's knees. Later, whenever we tried
  to meander on our inner tubes, we'd get lodged
    on the bottom. Seth, remember, no matter how we'd

kick and shove off, we'd just get lodged again?
  At most an afternoon would carry us a hundred feet
    toward the willows. We'd piss ourselves on purpose

just to feel the spirits of our warmth haloing out.
  And once, two bald men on the footbridge, bowing
    in the sky, stared down at us without a word.

THE MUSE

Today, shopping for fish
at the Piggly Wiggly,
I met for the first time
a woman of my grandmother's
generation, Mrs. Otto, who
by some unlikely coincidence
had read a few of my poems.
She wasn't impressed.

But before our introductions,
in the great tabernacle quiet
that is the smallest supermarket,
she and I stood awhile
quite close. Her ear leveled
at my elbow, we bellied up
to a freezer chest, together
looking down upon
the spread of salmon fillets.

What an orderly corner
of the world we saw, five
rectangles of tangerine flesh
vacuumed under cellophane
in styrofoam boats.
                    Immaculate.
Well, no. I came to see
one cut was blemished slightly—
a black hole puncture on this portion

of flesh, the wound arrayed
in a bruise gaining ground
unseen, putting out
purple ring, purple ring.
Mrs. Otto looked, too.
Yet, strangers as ever before,
neither she nor I would know
how fine a thing this was
so still between us:

O, this fish, a part of salmon,
bears such little resemblance
to the same-named creature
that spirits northwestern rivers.
This body netted, penned,
hosed, thrown, bludgeoned, flayed,
quartered, boarded, wrapped, and frozen,
then laid before us inside-out;
that now we might glimpse, it seems
—by what it lacks so profoundly
yet precisely—its divinity.

Then she said, "Hello,
excuse me, don't I know you?"
and asked for my name.

The name I gave, the sound
I carry, sounded different
than it had before.

In its six-syllable wake
I watched her rise before me,
heightened by new posture,
the look of a lone barn, dark-
windowed, splinter-boarded,
holding and holding
in prairieland wind.

With her hand still held
in mine, she delivered
this sentence: "I can't
help but notice, Mr. Carelli—
the Lord has never appeared
in any of your poems."

With that, Mrs. Otto
turned away, allowing me
but a single frame of silhouette
as she paused, wholly unhurried,
to bow before the freezer,
to catch a piece of fish, to lift it up.
And being held there herself
fluorescent in these every-
morning waters that are felt,
passed through, and never known,
she picked of the five, to take
and to eat, the rotten one,
the flesh most dead.

How strange. I probably
should have said thank you.

But then she left me,
shepherding her squeaky cart
to the end of the line, where
a poem extends a broken silence,
where faith resounds and finds
no end, where, between myself
and Mrs. Otto, a word I thought
I knew was lost.

THE CRUSADES

And now what shall become of us without any barbarians?
                                                    —Constantine Cavafy

In the plaza, tender with the light of candle lanterns,
    twelve Christians are murdered for their imaginations

of the wrong god . . . Please, god, I think, speeding off
    beneath the city, may that be my last day of work,

but the seat I'm stuck to slumps me toward tomorrow.
    In the twilight of the tunnel I dream of this tomorrow;

it's the one I always dream, the one I won't describe,
    the fine day for which I want no measure . . . Likewise

in history a smoke line appears, bronze above the desert
    hung atop clay roofs. Likewise a second plume soon

bruises the wind. Two, now three black flags lean east—
    the British bombarding Alexandria. As I walk home

the trees explode. They buckle slabs of sidewalk,
    dark hands lifting blaze leaves up the brownstones

to the boxes of sky on Joralemon. I cannot say why
    all of a sudden this happiness. Could be all my work

with poetry, though I'm not a poet yet. Could be weariness
    —my every morning ride up the same swift chutes

rising bright in rectangular blues of empty windows,
    and knowing each evening I'll retrace these shadows.

I'm hungry, which means our children are hungry,
    but there are no children; the streets are empty.

I realize nothing about this may sound like happiness.
    Still, as I stop with the trees and the city hums

with the distant rush of honey bees on expressways
    —and however dreadful or imagined it seems—

I believe the trees explode just the way it sounds.
    Their warmth on my face, I believe the grass-made

cracks in the streets burn too. What becomes of me
    when nothing terrible happens, and yet I see

a terrible beauty spiriting its embers to the awnings,
    blushing the very sky? With beauty Cavafy says

men sit expecting barbarians that never come through.
    He's wrong. They rush this poem's quiet plaza

as they rioted, merciless, in the poems of Cavafy
    whether he saw them or not. The trees explode.

And the mind sets off once more across the prairie
    between a dead bus hull and my building's stoop,

where the lit debris falls, scentless as evening mists
    fall, cool, erasing faraway capitals. It's that quick.

THE BUILDER

If I were called in to construct a religion
I would make use of lumber, and naturally
I would find the best lumber in the land.
There's no shame in wanting your religion
to last. If I'm building to accommodate the gods,
I figure the platform should be nice
and sturdy; the gods might be really heavy.
Besides, all kinds of people are sure to come
and climb all over it, wear the thing out.
Therefore, if I build in Wisconsin, I'll use oak;
in New England, ironwood. And in Paraguay
I hear there's a flowering tree called lapacho
with wood so rigid and heavy it outlives men.
I'd like to get my hands on some of that.

THE COLLAR

Methought I heard one calling, "Childe";
And I reply'd, "My Lord."
                    —George Herbert

Do I lie in bed and listen to the morning dove coo?
No, as again the men next door have started
without me. Alarm at dawn: chorus of percussions
tempoless, directionless. Shingles busted up,
their brittle plates dropped in avalanching fizzles
—all below my lazy golden curtains. Hammer falls
echoing syllables—*present, present*—a roll call.
So quickly I get up and put the kettle on the stove.

Late, guilty, a teacup in hand, I add a bag of soil,
a glug of primer, a shovel-full of white sand.
It's not the first time; the guys won't mind.
I've yet to meet this crew, or even see them, ever,
but there's a friendliness about these messengers
flailing crowbars and nail claws to pry loose
wrecked feathers of paint-bubbled asbestos.
Under moth masks their tongues are on the run
in a language my grandpa could speak in a jam,
though he never dared be overheard, afraid
to be mistaken for a liberal.
                              At the table now,
in my steel toes, and rubbing the rust from my knee,
I await the late whistle and review the schedule.

Today we'll strip the old fisherman's house
to inoculate the site for the demolition crew
set to arrive, ten strong, within the week.
When the teapot groans I lift it to its labor
with a grace unfathomable to laypersons. O,
but have mercy, for not until my fifth gulp
is it rendered unto me

                    that I'm not a carpenter
nor plumber, mason nor electrician, and there's
nothing wrong.

              I'm a guest in a hostel on a hill
named *Happy*—a Chilean vacation in my twenty-
fifth year. It's January, the dead of summer here.
I can go back to bed,

                back to Maria of Valparaíso,
whom I met in the park yesterday, who called out
"Americano" in lieu of my fine Christian name.
She's still asleep

             undisturbed
by my gallop out of bed
and the spooking of the sheets.

                  She knows of me
as little as she wears—this absolutely nothing
she said she prefers, even at the dinner table
eating empanadas.

             From the foot of the bed
the sound of her sleeping is the hilltops humming
in a glance above the city.

                 But as I lay me down
I go forth in penitence, my ear newly attenuated
by the real in the next noise heard

                      —There!
far off, another host of hammers—but from such
a distance it's impossible to know

                for sure

the story I hear: is it nails pounded in, building up;
or glass panes smashed, tearing down?

Voiceless but not songless,
                              a cadence floats up
on a brightening tide in the day-lit window
of her shirtless chest.

THE APOSTLES

—*for J. D.*

I sleep in, in the country of Chile, in the city
Valparaíso, in a hostel on a hill named *Happy*
on what becomes the windiest day of the year.
Already the gossamer curtains, as long as
women hung by their hair, gather the spirits
dancing in their dresses, flaring golden billows
over my bed, tickling me awake. So I awaken
knowing the only thing I want is to throw
rocks through the windows of La Sebastiana,
the most heavenly of Neruda's four homes.
What an absurd associative leap! I attempt
to dissuade myself, but have no more success
against myself than I would the west wind.
The wind today will only say shatter, shatter,
no matter my argument. "So what do ya think?"
I ask over tea and white bread. "It's stupid,"
you say, "and that's that." Today is destined to be
the anniversary of nothing. We take a walk—
the same walk we've walked together on each
of the last seven days, along the oxbow avenue
that wends the twenty-odd hills that bound
around the bay, tilting the city like an audience
applauding the Pacific. Nearby lean-tos flap
blades of rough-cut sheetmetal—stolen, I'm told,
from the wrecks of the most recent earthquake.

Loud as the gale you try, once again, to explain
how the tiny unpunctuated poems you've intended
to finish for seven years (and still fail) function.
"Can't hear you," I holler. You smile unhearing.
Your hood whips up. The front of a business
flings to the flock, cartwheeling over the cliff.
"I'm just glad to talk," I try to say. Glad at last
to skip Santiago, where I found my sister tangled
in a man who would manage to ruin her life
with just one month of abuse. "But it can also
be sweet," she'd say. "He's really not that bad . . ."
as she cried every morning in her glass of juice.
"So I skipped town and came here." I holler
and look for a nod, but you haven't received
a word, for a bird, a lark, is borne between us,
utter inertia, close as a housefly or the lowest
of the apples, wind-pinned in place. So startled
to appear among these men, it bucks against
the pins. Again it bucks but makes no headway.
Stitches of feather on the breast uproot and peel
away. I hear you hollering, "Dive! Dive! Dive!"
and know, for an instant, you speak as a god.
Let us order the bird into certainty, the ground,
some stationary welkin, knowing full well
what the lark cannot. To our right the city towers
tiny shacks. To our left, a downward slope
stacked until the buildings give way
to waterfront. A gust. Watch it. Above us
the silver ghettos are blowing apart.

DISCERNMENT

I'm no ladies' man, but somehow I took her.
It was Wednesday in a park called *Concepción*.
She was a stranger, local, Chilean, and I had just
awakened from a dream. She knew I was *gringo*
though I had always been mistaken for Argentine
because my hair is light and my nose Roman.
"Americano?" she asked. When I nodded she knelt
in the shade where I lay with feral Iberian worms.
"Wait. No," I started, but she squatted atop me
thumbing her underwear aside beneath her dress.
"What about those kids over there?" I pleaded
but she wouldn't heed. "Ooh," she cooed in Spanish:
"Americanos are famous—famous like Caesar,
Hitler, Pinochet—I really like that in a man."

THE CHANCE

I'm not greedy, but the night bear is.
Both of us come in the dark to your window.
You're dreaming, sleeping
mouth open;
the ripe yellow guavas in the window tree
must be in season. I love
ripe yellow guavas.
I don't know about that bear though.
Best be careful. Really, Honey,
not to be greedy, but
we better eat the guavas
while we have the chance.

IN ORDINARY TIME

Nothing came up, and the money ran out,
so I found a job in the neighborhood—
food service, a new joint called The Pie Shop.
My work is what you might call *whatever*—
"whatever sells the pies," my boss says . . .
Turns out I'm a natural. A Midwestern smile
proves to be a mighty *whatever*. The pies fly.
But we're talking savory (meat) not sweet pies
—no cherry, no pumpkin, no banana cream.
Sorry. No, ma'am, we don't have apple either.
No sweet ones. Sorry. Thanks for coming in.
Smile. Then, more often then not, they buy
a shepherd's anyway, or a mince and cheese.
Never before have I said I'm sorry so often.
Never before have I been so forgiven.

OCTOBER ADVENT

"Oh . . . hey . . . Honey
. . . do you need
some attention?"

This is Angie,
along whose hip
my hip is cupped;

this, her sunrise
mumble of the day,
responding to spirits,

for a moment ago
I'd elbowed up
to the uppermost

levels of bed. "Hey,"
I told her, "Hey . . .
babe . . . look . . .

it snowed."
But now I'm thinking,
need some attention?

what does snow have to do with me?
"No," I roll to the
window, pointing away

from my chest, away
from the center
of space. "Look,"

I whisper to no one
I know, as Angie
has already followed

my voice to her dreams.
I asked her to look,
traversing the glass,

but nothing is there,
for this kind of seeing
requires another.

Angie sees nothing,
and as she sees nothing,
I also have nothing

to see. Though
there is the sycamore
standing before me

in its yellow slicker,
alone and all too familiar,
astonished in snow

as if turned in a crowd
to glimpse the stranger,
whoever it was,

the holy man
whose passing hand
had brushed its own.

THE BEGATS

—in memoriam Merce Cunningham

First, there was movement in a clerestory window. Chaos.
    The heart. Reaching up of oak leaves: dance, wind, treetop.

And then that afternoon a wonder-man appeared among us.
    I mean on TV: a body come electric in the air ever briefly

caught, pale gull in the cathode rays. When I say *appeared*
    among us, among us, I long for precision, though that day

I lounged alone, avoiding chores, captaining an upstairs room
    of my parents' house through a bean field county seat.

When I say *in the air ever briefly* I mean I changed channels.
    The story goes like this: first, a man on stage leapt up

as a tree shaken into birds, larks, tongues; and now I arrive
    at work, The Pie Shop, outside of which I find a perfect apple

boot-smashed on the sidewalk, one step from the door. White
    once bound in emerald skin begetting winged articulations

in Brooklyn dark: bless this image of an apple. Bless the son-
    of-a-bitch who stomped it. How quickly we forget the lovely

way from there to here. Have I told you that our village name
  is a misnomer—that our pioneers were taken by the surname

of some Frenchman, but the charter was drafted by a penman-
  avant-garde whose calligraphy baffled the clerk at the State.

Our *Poynette*—it turns out—is *Pauquette* misbegotten. So
  chance was a root in the land my mother shaped, kneeling

in the garden, spade in hand, beckoning furrows for tomato
  seeds. And when she beckoned me, *Tony*, out to my chores,

among the words *knee* and *toe*, *tone* and *E*, I heard
  a name I knew and went. Isn't this how I'm carried

through my days? Wasn't the bulk of my grace once simply
  those buckets of soil I carried across the garden? Wasn't

my grace the weight of the earth in my hands? Isn't all legacy
  brevity? That dancer—what did he look like? I can tell you

he had curly hair, a shock, and when he moved (or stopped)
  his limbs held court. His body, as I saw it, was a lens

lit from within, a projector churning out light on the wall
  of my grandfather's basement, his flesh the flicker of images

—all my family's favorites—carried forth. And his head
  was buoyed, marshaled by air, not shouldered by his body.

But I changed the channel. Did I even see the dancer's name
  was Cunningham? Of course not. Yet so wholly, so fully,

a poem can hold the name of every bird I never noticed
  as it banked above the garden, shouldering selves, moment

to moment, in downstrokes of sunlight, upstrokes of wind.
   Hallelujah, though, if we ourselves carry anything at all.

As I stand before you at The Pie Shop, preparing you pies,
   the music I hear all around me sounds nothing like the city

I imagined this morning. And this dancer that I never knew . . .
   Well, here I am, all lit up, a bit surprised to sing the next line:

Hey, there should be only one church—maybe, it would be
   better in this city. There are more churches here than

people I know. Grand stone castles growing on the avenues
   wings and additions. The outlying branches' smaller steeples:

just think of the churches. Some simple houses where even
   the children inside haven't realized they, themselves, are slowly

becoming churches. Big old beauties. Our upward attentions.
   Churches of the future, churches of the past. Today I found

what looked like a nice one, catching the sunrise with trees
   full of birds, oaks as heavenly as anything you've seen.

But later, on a billboarded corner, the ringing comes on
   so heavy, so many bells bong so many towers, it makes me

a tired man. I wonder, must I always be this man? Just think:
   one church. Things could be different, better, if there were

one church here . . . But now you must have heard the music
   change. Now I sing because I want no church at all.

What remains in the morning but surprise? Prayer? Dance is
   forever, I'm told, a fugitive lover. *It gives you nothing*

back. No manuscripts to store away. No paintings to show
    on walls and maybe hang in museums . . . Nothing but

that single fleeting moment when you feel alive. It is not
    for unsteady souls. So I pray: grant me this, another morning

to stay where I am—here in Brooklyn, working at The Pie Shop,
    selling pies. I've come to like it. Grant me this, O lord,

but do not bully me, do not stop by, not even disguised
    as the woman I love. I'm not fooled. I glimpse a savior here,

begotten every morning in the stock of frozen dough
    bagged in fours, balanced in spires to the great heights

of the icebox. And I see the same pies become flesh
    as I heat them, swaddle them, hand them to commuters.

All these images I tend tend to diminish. So leave me be,
    especially at times like this: before we open, before

the sun hits, before the oven bird begins to sing paradise.
    O lord, O unsteady. The empty café sounds its bell,

as if endless—brief as the endlessness of a generous heart
    —six black chairs unlit, space made new by absence.

THE SHEPHERD

It's instinct. Days when the mercury dropped
  precipitously before a summer thunderstorm
    the entire herd of Holstein cows, thirty or so,
      lay down, huddling in the fenced field corner
nearest the highway. There's an oak tree there,
a big old brawling lifelong farmer of a tree,
    that offered the creatures some certainty
      whenever the storms would harass them.

On such days, when Dick Balfanz and I
  came driving toward this common cattle spot,
    he'd straighten in his seat, awaiting his moment.
      We'd have a stack of panels headed for some
fast-food joint, a real shit gig, and no reason
to hurry on. And so it was that he and I,
    in preparation for this rainy day ritual,
      would come to rest at the southwest bend.

Then he'd crank down his window, so that rain-
  drops might jewel his wrist, a tiny moonlit field,
    beyond which, now curious, I saw the cattle shift
      slightly in their tight plot. And finally, those days,
Dick, looking for humor, leaned through the window
with one shoulder bared, soaked, so that his head
    might fit the opening, so that he might holler out
      into the storm, "Get a job, you lazy bastards."

LECTIO DIVINA

If the item presented is a chicken pie
    I will see the lord. But let me see Angie,

and let me see the Great Red Spot of Jupiter, too,
    for each of these things are contained therein.

In love the only order of business is attention,
    a difficult attention to the most distant image

and also to your meal, both at once. Immediately
    this truth reminds me of The Pie Shop.

As I tire at the end of an eleven-hour shift,
    the windowed room that spreads before me

flickers—though I see the keys of a sleeping
    register, a stack of square napkins spiraled

for a certain wow effect, three square tables
    and six black chairs lifting six good patrons

as another night will come between us—
    the scene becomes marbles, and my eye,

the steelie. Which is to say I'm happy. I love marbles
    glinting even as their constellation shatters

to the corners. The door blows open; a beauty appears
    —a silver-haired girl has entered the shop.

She's looking for help, but needing some time.
    "Gimme a sec to see what you got . . . Yeah,

can I get a couple of whatever's most popular?"
    And so I return to the arithmetic of *pie plus pie*

and *what's her change.* What is love if not
    the aptitude for refreshment? This girl is not

the focus of my days, but is her apparition any less
    a part of love than the initial chicken pie?

Sure, at the end of eleven hours I simply want it
    to stop, but I'll stand in back, near the oven,

where it's warm as a summer night, a baseball night,
    and I'll think of nothing in particular—a nothing

that becomes a game at Yankee Stadium, a blowout.
    There beyond the outfield, high above the wall,

a host of flags float in the sky, stuck on poles
    that never bow, the way fishtails stick to trout

that face the current—another customer enters
    from the street—absolutely still, but flourishing

in the water of the wind. The Great Red Spot
    of Jupiter, at such a distance, may blossom

to be a carnation a customer left on the counter.
    The lord, I posit, is a baseball doorstop, bolted

to the floor. And the wind, yes, the gasp from the oven,
    a rumor of ten thousand pastries—Angie, that's you.

THE HOURS

"Tony, hit the lights," He says. "Hit the windows."
My boss is nervous. What can I do?
It's his big day—extended hours at The Pie Shop,
our inaugural opening at dawn, closing at ten.
"This is when the money starts to roll," I'm told.

The first dawn of my twenty-ninth year, and still
I'm staggered by the godliness of sunlight,
how its bands assuage my skin from wrist to elbow
as I spiral clouds of Windex on the glass. Old light
turned down 16th Street from my left to my right

smashes like a sycamore
felled on the steeple of Farrell's Bar and Grill.
No one's there to hear the shook glass ring,
no one but the Mexican who busses from Harlem
to mop the holy tack from the bootprint floor.

I wonder. Doesn't he, despite himself, love
this terrible work: clearing a path of tile
to call an unknown patron from the stoop
to his stool, from there to the men's room,
from the men's room to midnight, every night?

Let there be no doubt. Sunrise is salvation
on certain streets of Brooklyn, if only
you can manage to ignore it. Keep a hand on a rag

or a broom or a wheel. "Whad'ya say, Tony?
Should we do the pie display?" This means

quickly I should rid the glass of fingers.
"Should we sweep the floor, too?"
The floor will be unburdened of crumbs.
"Should we stack the bags of coffee in the shape
of a pyramid?" The bags will be stacked by me.

Should I want something more?
Yes, but the upswing of each dark task stalls out.
And each dark task stalled out turns me back, and I fall
down the arc of momentum
to the heavens: this wall of windows;

this sidewalk,
salt-burnt, gleaming down the hill
to the subway hole; this side street
above which elm trees look the other away
as they lift imperceptibly toward the flame.

"Tony, get the pies."
I glance at my grandfather's watch: quarter
past seven. And the first of the commuters,
a silver-haired girl—the first, I pray,
of thousands—appears at the door.

AGNUS DEI

A true *murmuration* is a hundred thousand starlings
    tumbling a shadow in the sky above the fields. *Cloud*

crowds in; then, *leviathan*. But whenever that notion
    of brilliance appears—that briefly-collected, *my lord!*, silver

belly of wind—and when all we have to do to know its heft
    is take an evening stroll along the roadside fences; trace

the hand-cut squares of mint, peas, beans, tobacco; turn
    to the hum-honk of Interstate 90; and lift up our eyes,

we find the word for this glory, the word for this world,
    taken away. But maybe not the word for what we came upon

next: the eight-year-old Mexican, swaddled in a gunnysack
    jacket, of sorts, and hung from the span of Kent Road Bridge.

Maybe this word comes and comes to stay—a terminology
    built of artifacts, a gilded evidence of an earlier scene

no one can see—though who could survive its utterance?
    Rope, corded, not very thick; an impeccably-fashioned

fisherman's clinch; black-bottom feet flexed in like worms,
    two worms dangled to gushes and cusses of traffic. And

the laughing, that bizarre sound. Was the boy laughing?
    I return to the starlings, return to the starlings, because

the marvel of their never-tangled arcs, at first, misguided us
    to skygaze. We stopped on the bridge, *good god!*, under-

rumbled by the honk and lift of car exhaust gusts. Later
    we knelt on concrete, mouthing gently nonsense Spanish

to the boy the patrolmen had hoisted up. Earlier, it was Friday,
    Labor Day weekend, getting on toward dusk. We were headed

to the Millers' for fish fry. We thought nothing of the flickers
    of familiar eyes missing in the fields: the turkey and crane

erased from alfalfa, the workers in their ever-lowered hats
    disappeared, or the lone trophy buck blotted out in the corner

of fresh-cut corn. We walked out onto the bridge, but then,
    like I said: the murmuration. Fifty yards above our heads

are birds in heaven: a peloton of vapor, exaltation undulating
    in and out of view, condensation bluffs flashing sudden

acres, coal-plant smokestack blossoms in the lurch—all
    birds. Now, imagine this thunder is wings; this darkness

is bodies, spontaneity is flesh, and not the simple matter of dust
    lifted, dispersing. Then, the laughing. How is it that we even

use words anymore? *Exaltation* is never made of starlings.
    No *blossoms* ever opened this particular darkness; neither

did *smoke*. And *laughing* is less and less the proper gospel
    for the sound we couldn't hear—a boy's voice. We couldn't

hear a word above the din. And yet: the word nonetheless.
    We looked down from the edge, tried to say what we saw.

The little one wasn't singing. He wasn't bleating. But wasn't
    silent. He wasn't. And there, below, what did you see?

I saw carnations, fresh white ones, freshly unfurled, fresh
    as forgetting—the widening eyes of passengers flashing

upward, unbidden, unopposed; blooms as if grasping at
    the holy light itself. And only light. The road rushed white

with carnations. There was no catching that awe with our
    shadow hands. There was no stopping that pummeling up.

THE BROOKLYN HEAVENS

It is difficult to say why nobody looks at anybody here.
On a path I bend and pass among a couple dozen strangers.
Each of them is holy like the dying trees that bend away
to show their faces to the pond, way out in the middle,
where the pond has no eyes, and nobody can stand to see.
Holy, I guess, but people I pass without a word or thought
are no better than gods, because again I've lost my chance
to speak to them, and now they talk behind my back.

EVANGELICAL

Six months open. A smile
six months long. One half-year
of "Welcome to The Pie Shop."
So busy we've extended hours
and bumped prices (a shepherd's
is going for five twenty-five).
We added a salad with three
kinds of lettuce and recruited
extra staff. Two Sundays ago
we got blurbed in *The Times*,
and a neighborhood gazette
has followed suit. Incidentally,
I appear in the second article:
"a kind-eyed guy named Tony."
Then, later on, the reviewer,
whose name I can't remember,
enthuses, "Stroke your senses
at 211 Prospect Park West"
—that's our address. Great.

But despite the evidence of space,
and of time, and of experience,
there are those of our neighbors
who will enter the shop, still
unconvinced the shop exists.
You'd think a host of empty walls
were being swung between us,

obstructing providence, rendering
our glass façade opaque.

"Yes—" I told the man
who happened through our door
on Thursday night, a union man
according to his foam-front hat,
a Yanks fan according to his jacket
"—we exist, sir. I'm working here."
I raised my arms to cue the menu.
I traced along the custom lights.
Then, as if it proved I'm not a ghost,
I showed the wall of windows;
I pointed to the benches on the sidewalk
outside, as they knelt, ignoring our attention,
staring up the towers of clouds.

"But I live here," he told me,
and was angry, strangely so.
"I grew up on Seventeenth,"
His hands winged up to align
the stripes that pinned his collar.
"I've never seen you," he said,
"and I walk by this corner
every morning, every night."

BIRTHDAY

> Here the serpent-son,
> *Apollo's offspring, came to land, put on*
> *His heavenly form again, and to the people*
> *Brought health and end of mourning. The old god*
> *Came to our shrines from foreign lands, but Caesar*
> *Is god in his own city.*
>
> —Ovid, *Metamorphoses*, book XV

Ooh, the vision comes and goes, and again it appears
the poet was right. There *is* something out there mounting up
beneath the surface . . . This morning the lake is invisible.

We've come to the harbor on my twenty-sixth birthday
with hopes to see the big ship set to arrive from Japan.
It will not be carrying back triumphant men—just better cars.

The longshoremen stand out the length of the dock in blazing jumpers,
waiting for the dawn arrival already delayed an hour
by this fog in my father's hometown.

A hundred-or-so stand near us in the infinity hallway;
a few close enough to reveal noses and hands, Italian-looking,
like my grandfather's, and father's, and mine (though less and less so).

Kenosha is hideous behind us, cloaked by this cloud that hangs
on the pigeons flushed out: the last exhalation of the auto assembly.
We wait at the base of the docks, and talk about the White Sox,

not the Roman Empire. My father and I stare right at it, but talk baseball.
Do you know what I mean? Further out in the distance,
the trundling distance that you, my father, can't see—

even if you'd stop talking baseball a minute and look
—another hundred men settle in, stretching necks and backs,
to laze in varied stations of disappearance, and are gone.

There, in the Senate of the even greater distance,
Caesar is made a god to account for his brilliant succession
—his boys, who, in turn, give the kingdom slowly away.

And then I see it—don't I?—vague in the flocks of what
promised to be a mighty ship, a mound spooks up
gaining huge ballast, riding high in the fog. It breaks

through the surface of the lake with a hush, and then, yes,
I see the eye, a swollen mirror, staring right back, seeing me.
Clearly the freighter is nowhere near. Knowing nearly nothing

about ships, we know no one would risk this run in the fog.
Why don't we speak of it? Dad, everywhere in Ovid a god
pursues us. Do you see it, but know of something truer?

Do you see, at least, that Kenosha is hideous?
When you stare at the lake do you see it's my birthday;
that it's me in the harbor? Do you see me coming in?

Were there times in your life when you knew
the kingdom was over? Were there times when you saw
what your father could not?

SERMON

The poet is a liar.
　　　—Fernando Pessoa

Every morning we would hoist Victor's father
　from the moist sheets, holding him for a third
　　to sponge his flanks and milk-sack thighs.
　　　"Put your elbow under the shoulder," Victor
　　　　instructed. "If his eyes open, you speak to him."
　　　　　One day a doctor interrupted our ritual.
　　　　　　"Look: I think your father smiles," he said.

And turning back, we couldn't help believing.
　No matter our suspicion of the doctor's simple savvy,
　　nor the fact of a familiar face inverted, inert,
　　　we were children again, bodiless, it seemed,
　　　　gathered and held kite-like above our father's head,
　　　　　lifted up to pluck the last armful of apples—
　　　　　　the best ones, he said: the ones he couldn't reach.

ORIGINAL SIN

I work all morning, writing bad lines
like *Valparaíso glass drips in windows,*
so looking out the leaves are bubbled.

At noon a new wind swishes and flashes.
The gasman rolls uphill drumming bells
tax-ticket-tax ticket-ticket-ticket-tax.

As the gasman rolls uphill drumming bells
the pane falls free of my bedroom window.
Whoa, it doesn't fall slashing like glass falls;

rather like a loose envelope: skyward at first,
then, sheets, looped, glinting at the mercy
of gravity's superior, the superior of space,

as a boy is thrown by his father overhead.
The boy's father's face, withered away . . .
blooms back. "Up," the boy begs, "Up, Dad, Up."

Today, looking out, I find the city falling
down. A kind of rush the eye can't
quite catch. I'm so excited, so excited.

FAITH

The Italian way with the knife is done.
But what about this sleeveless, rickety LP
at the bottom of my father's dusty stacks?
—Alessandro Moreschi, *The Last Castrato,*
The Complete Vatican Recordings.
What takes me at this tender age of twenty-eight,
what spirits me and drags me to the attic,
unearths the turntable, restarts the record,
what dials down the volume knob to 1?
Ave Maria. Just imagine: this voice,
the last of its kind, so the only of its kind—
limitless pitch, limitless in time. *Hallelujah.*
And meanwhile, outside, a century later,
my father finishes mowing the lawn.

INCARNATION

If and when the others come,
ramble through Poynette,
and happen down the park
from Mill Street, the swell of the herd
ruining mosquito screens
on Grace's porch, collapsing
jungle gyms, the birch, and birdhouses
as they advance,

they'll be channeled through these old willows, one by one,
to the Rowan Creek Bridge.

Our entire nomadic race
will pass.

And if they rush from the north,
trample the softball field,
one chasing down
a well-hit fly ball
to left-center—or in winters,
as they migrate south
for more temperate weather—
they'll be forced into a single line here:

each
to train
ginger

steps across
slick
gnarled
planks.

But you and I—
    we walk down the hill to the footbridge
        whenever there's nothing else to do.

These are full afternoons
given to standing
at the halfway point,
thinking of—No: waiting for
—what?

The hovering
helicopter
seedpods whirl
mapletops
to the creekbed.

Trout emerge for scraps of toast.
When walkers come,
we let them pass,
then back to our position in the middle.

To stand this way, shoulder
to shoulder, belly-up
to the rail. To feel togetherness,
hold absolutely still, quiet
between syllables.

If you ever get bored,
just climb the crosshatch
and lean across the rail, bowing
to start and stop a somersault
in brushes of leafy air—a long

fall to the bedrock
deferred. Stomach
hardened to hardwood
so that you teeter-totter
without pain. A pivot on the railing,
your arms wing out, shoulders forward,
unburdening your sneaker soles.
Now, pretend you're a sprinter
                           winning a race
where everyone tries to keep pace with the fluid rushing
impossible earth.

        Ooh!
        a nudge, now—
        a breeze blew,
        and a fireball sinking into Fireman's Park.

The time
come to climb
the hill, to go
back home.

NO, EURIPIDES

"No, Euripides.
Not again.
No more.

Don't let another god appear
in the theater.
It's so disappointing.

When the gods are called, and they come
and prance around like the bodies of men,
they're ruined for me.

Let them be wonderful,
not pigeons in sunlight,
nor the dumb sea confusing Ithacan sailors.

Stop pestering those strange creatures.
We may find someday
we need them."

YAHWEH

"Use fresh words," I was told, "and speak clearly."
Then my masters insisted, "All of poetry
    has but two subjects," one of which was love.
        The other, though equally impressive,
            I can never recall. There was love
                and the other thing. "Neither of which, boy,"
                    I was warned, "should we mention explicitly."

However, my mother said love all the time.
    In the words of Plain Jane she whispered,
        "I love the spring," as the farm-proffered green
            flickered virtues through the pickup windows.
                Love meant something like *Look closely, Tony,*
                and goldenrod becomes more GOLDENROD!
                    But then of course my mother passed away.

APPLES FOR THOREAU

> *. . . for if he has lived sincerely, it must have been in a distant land to me. Perhaps these pages are more particularly addressed to poor students.*
>
> —from *Walden*

I shouldn't even look.
The fifteen hundred pheasants lit on the field are stuck in cages
as they have been every year.

A field east of town is set aside for game birds, nets
draped over wood trusses, posts and crossbars stained bark gray.
I tell you, Henry, something's wrong.

These eyes.
Some mornings the light driving down
deliberate on the acres of fabric has convinced me of fog.

Fog, I think, and this familiar peace rolls through me all day.
Tricks. It's the light.
The same sun in the evenings will color everything
with a richness I can't explain.
No.
There's nothing like it in old paintings, nothing like it in foreign lands.

Last night, over my drive home
the sky was unimaginable, cloudscape, thin moon.

The land around the highway darkened,
expected, to the wooded corners of the clearing.

On these nights, when I pass the pheasant field, I've come to expect it
—a moment when I miss the nets washed out
by this particular trick
of light, and the pheasants
emerge, out there, unfettered, simply waiting

—McIntoshes—fifty acres scattered with apples.
I'm certain of it. This is not our place.
I mean the world.

JERUSALEM

There was indeed on earth, so long as it was needed, a symbol and foreshadowing image of this city, which served the purpose of reminding men that such a city was to be, rather than making it present; and this image was itself called the holy city . . .

—St. Augustine

_____'s father falters in the state hospital.
  105 degrees. No air conditioning. Bedsores
    the size of soap dishes. The doctor on vacation
      in X or Y. An early knock-knock and the nurse
        not there. But a new syringe of tepid serum
left on the tile outside his door. And always
  a note with a one-word instruction scribbled
    in the language of butchers: *shoulder, rump,*
      stomach. The needle. *You* do it. Even worse,
        _____ had visited the States. Where *none of this*

would ever happen. That night, as the fever peaked,
  eleven cucarachas hollered to one another o'er
    the chasm. This is how it was: fear, then death,
      then a biblical anger. The next afternoon,
        the story goes, I called _____ a coward in Spanish
after having heard him with the doctor's daughter,
  the two of them singing skyward like a kite
    and a helicopter—an unforgivable trespass,
      because, at the time, _____ was married
        to my sister. My lord. Two days later I flew home.

THE CRUCIFIXION

The blast blasted blubber beyond all believable bounds.
—Paul Linnman of KATU-TV

What now? In a forty-five-foot, eight-ton mound, the dead sperm whale
  washed a question ashore: *once given, how do you go about giving god back?*

So isn't it shameful that we, still unknowing, will answer with dynamite?
  Monkish distraction: this quick digging the pits beneath the enormous

bearded flank, handkerchiefs guarding our faces from the real work at hand,
  which is looking—isn't it?—a difficult looking at slipping away, an end

larger than ours, decay. That's the task we all return to, however briefly,
  when the easier business of shovels is done. Backs on dunes, sandwiches

on our sandy laps, we try to watch the blubbered hall go on not moving.
  There's not much to see. Early clouds the size of countries ride over us

and slip off unrememberable. New questions flock. Spirals of terns and gulls
  collapse from the sky to pick at the carcass staunch as a church. A god

has come. What will make it matter? Fire, nails, camera, action. As if
  we make the unimaginable more: we plant the charge, we run the cables.

THE LORD'S PRAYER

You can't fake it. You know when I fail
      to achieve the expected: palm the becoming-
            comatose bullfrog, legs collapsing as they may,
and *chuck* it (we used to say) high as you can.

Let it fly stone-like to the skylight in the low
      dome of fog—another requirement of the game:
            a foggy day and a bullfrog and you, Vincent.
The old code goes back and forth between us

as we take our turns, childhood pals, engaged
      by the game we once called Kamikaze—now,
            a nameless ceremony. Nameless not because
a boy's play calcifies in a man's conviction;

not because, despite our promise, you've become
      a mid-rank fighter pilot, and I a minor poet;
            and not because it's too unpleasant to name
what brings to hand that astonished muscle

only to leave it, later, sprawled on the current.
      The perfect toss sends the critter shattering
            for an instant, beyond fog, into the invisible.
Disappearance is success. Once you said, "My insides

tickle whenever it happens," and so I know
      you've been tickled five times, and I three.

That's the score; the score matters little.
The name is gone because we're *from* here,

and, being native, cannot visit how it is
    that an urge to which we tend tends to us—
        how we are cruel, inscrutable, indefensible,
yet holy. How we send up bodies of praise from

our right hand, only to gather eventual elegies—
    flesh stunned still as words—in our left.
        Once again the center of the heavens
is earth. We've thrown as high as we can

for as long as we can remember, only to await
    some return: a revelation, plummet, explosive
        splash. So it is that two grown men
may stand again in stillness, awaiting word,

friends who glimpse for seconds at a time
    earth as it is in heaven, ankle-deep
        in Rowan Creek with eyes uplifted,
reflecting the fog to the fog itself.

THE DISCIPLES

At least I have, I think, this companionship.
On account of the impending blizzard
the friendly tender at the friendly pub
lines up free pints all night long.
We take the golden ore and leave the glass.
We take the copper ore and leave the glass.
We even take the heavy iron ore. Then,
at two o'clock on Tuesday morning
Ovid and I, sole patrons of the night,
head for home from the corner bar.
But home is nowhere near this corner.
Suddenly it's clear: there's no safe place.
I'm too drunk to find the truck, and Ovid
the Roman becomes barbaric in Wisconsin,
charging always into what he cannot know—
using the flash of high Latin, for example,
in a bid to impress a laid-off farmhand,
our last chance for a lift. Ovid, full of grace,
you'll never survive a night in this snow. So,
when the drifts take your legs and you call out,
may I know enough to know it's too late,
that the time has come to leave you behind—
those heroic feet in sandals, dancing in agony.

SURE

Do you think that a merely metaphorical resurrection would have
been enough for Archbishop Desmond Tutu?

—Jim Wallis

Rowan Creek,
    so high, so still,

there's no forgetting
    the years of us

damming the flow:
    text, memory.

Two thousand years
    made slow as glass—

but, ooh, spooked,
    a rainbow trout

glimmering off,
    already gone,

to where the water
    so full of glimmer

becomes sky
    wobbling branches

below the sky
   we call the heavens.

That glimmer there
   was not the lord,

but still the lord
   may be the glimmer.

AMEN

When she played piano
she nodded her head,
a branch bent down

in the rhythm's wind.
Beginning of measures,
herald of crescendo:

it also meant *Yes*
whenever her sight-reading
slipped, then regained—

Yes—the musical line.
As sails of a clipper
gain on the brink—

the metronome mast
bobbing, bowing,
approaching the sill

of a vanishing point
—she disappeared,
appeared again,

then disappeared.
Even now
I see my mother

where she's not—
kneeling in the drum
of a shadowed barn

otherwise empty.
Where's the horse?
The mare—hungry—

has trodden across
to the neighbor's field.
She's already nipped

every last promise
from the reachable branches
of his cherry tree.

Trouble:
the horse, the cherries,
the ship, the sea

—her body so eager
on the bench like a simile
happy in the sun.

But cast in shade
her chin would dip.
My chin dipped too.

My chin still dips
as a dolphin's does,
nosing up into one

glass sky and down
into others reflected,
as seen on TV.

When she played piano
my ear was a blossom
to the moon of her shoulder

—I mean, I listened hard
but never knew when
the time had come

to flip the page.
And in the meantime
I've taken a small

cut in wages; said yes
to a desk in the basement.
I look for the nod,

the last of the many,
the *Turn, please,*
to the Coda. Mom,

I nod to the signs, I
nod to that song, I nod
to the devil himself.